Our Dad Is Getting Better

Alex, Emily, and Anna Rose Silver

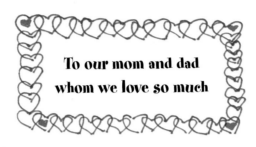

To our mom and dad
whom we love so much

Published by the
American Cancer Society
Health Promotions
1599 Clifton Road NE
Atlanta, Georgia 30329 USA

Printed in the United States of America
5 4 3 2 1   07 08 09 10 11

Designed by Martha Benoit

Library of Congress Cataloging-in-Publication Data
Silver, Alex.
 Our dad is getting better / Alex, Emily, and Anna Rose Silver.
    p. cm.
 ISBN 978-0-944235-86-7
 1. Cancer—Chemotherapy—Juvenile literature. I. Silver, Emily. II.
Silver, Anna Rose. III. Title.

 RC271.C5S52 2007
 616.99'4061—dc22

                                    2007014177

For more information about cancer, contact your American Cancer Society at 1-800-ACS-2345 or **www.cancer.org**

For bulk sales, please e-mail the American Cancer Society at **trade.sales@cancer.org**

EDITOR
Jill Russell

MANAGING EDITOR
Rebecca Teaff

BOOK PUBLISHING MANAGER
Candace Magee

DIRECTOR, BOOK PUBLISHING
Len Boswell

STRATEGIC DIRECTOR, CONTENT
Chuck Westbrook

Our Dad Is Getting Better

Alex, Emily, and Anna Rose Silver

This is a special day. It's Dad's last session of chemotherapy. Chemotherapy is a kind of medicine, also called "chemo," that makes you feel yucky, but it helps get rid of cancer. Our dad had cancer. But at last, after months and months of treatment, he is finally going to be done. We surprise him with a new watch and tell him, "This watch means it's time to start healing." We are all really happy about chemotherapy ending and healing beginning.

Even though Dad has had his last chemo treatment, he isn't feeling much better yet. He is very tired all the time and tells us that he can't do a lot of things he used to do. Staying at home makes Dad feel bored, but he is still too sick to go to work. All the people at school and in our neighborhood know that Dad was sick with cancer.

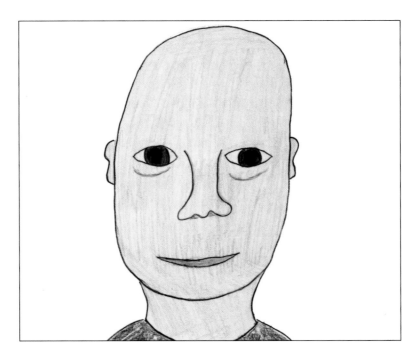

Today Dad had a checkup with the doctor. Although the worst part of the cancer treatment is over, the doctor wants him to keep taking some medicine. While Dad and Mom were gone, Grandma came over to baby-sit. We played some fun games with Grandma, but we missed Dad.

Dad's doctor tells him he should exercise more by taking walks. Dad says that we should all try to walk at least 10,000 steps every day. Now we go on lots of family walks. Dad wears a pedometer, a small machine that counts the number of steps a person takes. He is happy that everyone in the family is walking more, and he is happy that we are all getting healthier!

After Dad finished chemotherapy, people stopped bringing us dinner. So Dad and Mom started cooking again. Dad tells us that we should try to eat lots of fruits and vegetables every day. At first, this seemed hard and we didn't like it, but now we are used to it. We like fruits better than vegetables!

It takes a long time for Dad's hair to start to grow back. After a few weeks, he begins to get some hair, but it's really short. He is still tired, so he goes to bed early. Dad goes to bed earlier than anyone else. He needs a lot of rest. Mom helps us get ready for bed, and she says that someday Dad will feel better.

"Having cancer and recovering from cancer is very stressful," Dad says. That's why he meditates every day. Sitting quietly and meditating helps Dad get rid of stress and feel better. He says that we can try meditating, too. Sometimes we try it when we are having trouble falling asleep. We know how hard cancer has been on Dad, so we are always quiet when he meditates.

Dad is starting to feel better, so he begins to take us to do some fun things. He takes us apple picking at a local farm. Our whole family goes, and it's really fun. Everyone loves picking apples. Later, when we get home, our aunt helps us bake an apple pie with the fruit we picked. It's great when Dad takes us fun places!

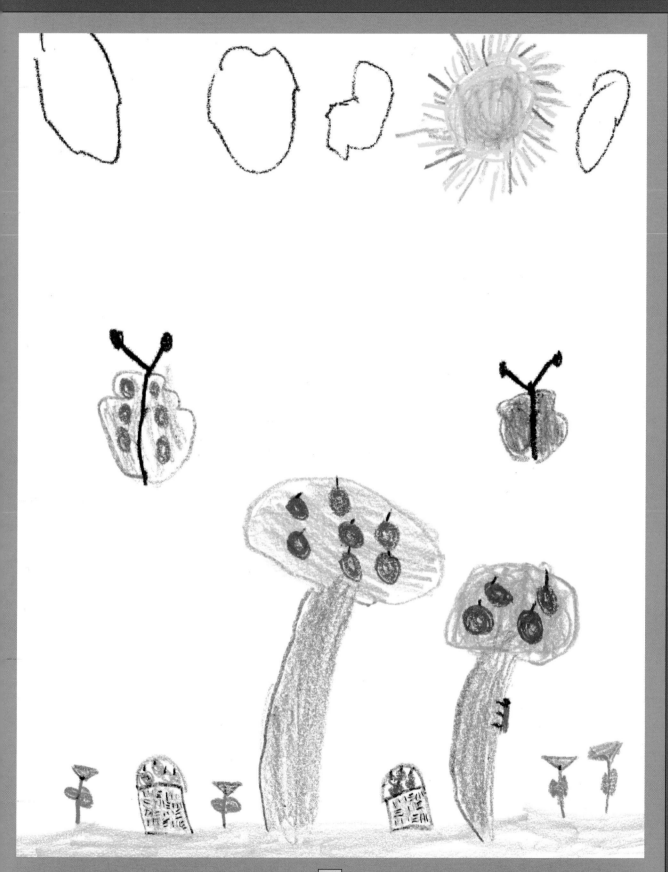

Although Dad is getting better, we still worry that the cancer might come back. When we ask Dad if his cancer will ever come back, he says he doesn't think it will. If it does, then the doctors and nurses will help him all over again. If Dad got cancer again, we'd be sad, but we know he would get as much help as possible.

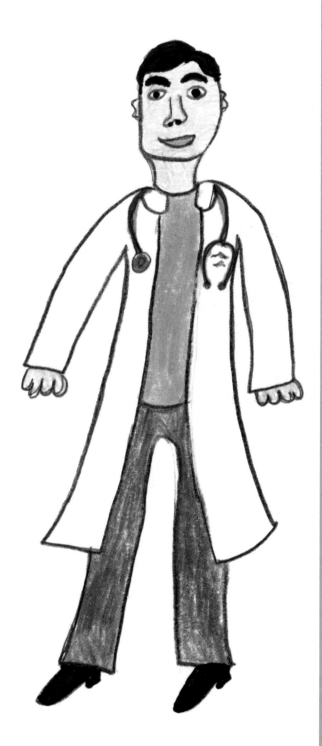

Today is Dad's birthday! He is feeling better, so Mom takes him out to eat at a restaurant. He gets dressed up in his nice clothes. They have a fun time talking, and the food is really good!

When Dad got sick, we had to cancel a family vacation we had planned with his side of the family who live far away. Everyone wanted to go, but we knew it would be too hard for Dad. So now that he is feeling better, we are going on a different vacation. We are happy to see our grandparents, our cousins, and our aunts and uncles. We all go to an amusement park and eat popcorn and cotton candy. The rides are really fun!

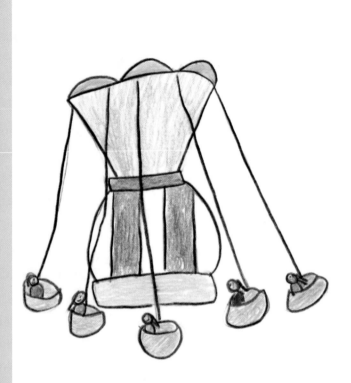

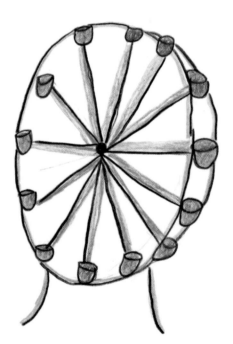

Dad says that it is time for him to go back to work. He finally feels well enough. On his first day returning to work, we all wake up early to help him get ready. Everyone agrees that this is an exciting day! Dad gives us each a big hug, and then we say goodbye as he leaves.

Our whole family wants to help raise money to cure cancer. One way we help is by walking in the Relay For Life®. Relay For Life is a wonderful event where you walk day and night around a track. People light special candles, called luminaria. Some candles make up words like "Hope."

There is also a survivors' walk, where cancer survivors like Dad walk around the track. Anyone can go to the Relay For Life—kids, families, friends—anyone. The walk raises a lot of money to help people with cancer, and it's fun to do!

It's another special day! This marks the one-year anniversary of when Dad was diagnosed with cancer. We celebrate by baking him a cake and having ice cream for dessert. Dad is still healing, but has come a long way since he got sick and is almost totally better.

Dad tells us that cancer is a terrible disease, and it hurts people a lot. But he also says that people who have had cancer can recover. This means that their lives go back to how they were before—almost. He says that life is never exactly the same after cancer, but we can still be happy!

Dad has shown us that it might be difficult at times to recover from cancer, but you can get through it. Our dad had a really big problem, but now he is feeling much better. We are all really happy that our dad is getting better!

About the Authors

Alex, Emily, and Anna Rose Silver live near Boston,
Massachusetts. Emily and Anna Rose drew the illustrations
for this book, and Alex wrote most of the text. Emily and
Anna Rose also helped write the book. Their mom is a
doctor and a cancer survivor. The Silver kids wrote and
illustrated this book as a companion to their book *Our Mom
Is Getting Better*. They are grateful for the opportunity to
share their cancer experience with other families.